WHEREBY THE LEAVES HAVE FALLEN

A Memoir

WHEREBY THE LEAVES HAVE FALLEN

A Memoir

Barbara Hegger-Romero

© 2023 by Barbara Hegger-Romero
All Rights Reserved
No part of this book may be reproduced in any form or by any electronic or mechanical means including information storage and retrieval systems without permission in writing from the publisher, except by a reviewer who may quote brief passages in a review.

Sunstone books may be purchased for educational, business, or sales promotional use. For information please write: Special Markets Department, Sunstone Press, P.O. Box 2321, Santa Fe, New Mexico 87504-2321.
Printed on acid-free paper
∞
eBook 978-1-61139-693-5

Library of Congress Cataloging-in-Publication Data

Names: Hegger-Romero, Barbara, 1947- author.
Title: Whereby the leaves have fallen : a memoir / Barbara Hegger-Romero.
Description: Santa Fe : Sunstone Press, [2023] | Summary: "The autobiography of a mother and grandmother at the age of 75"-- Provided by publisher.
Identifiers: LCCN 2022056757 | ISBN 9781632934642 (paperback) | ISBN 9781611396935 (epub)
Subjects: LCSH: Hegger-Romero, Barbara, 1947- | Catholic women--Biography. | LCGFT: Autobiographies.
Classification: LCC BV4527 .H439 2023 | DDC 282.092 [B]--dc23/eng/20221209
LC record available at https://lccn.loc.gov/2022056757

WWW.SUNSTONEPRESS.COM
SUNSTONE PRESS / POST OFFICE BOX 2321 / SANTA FE, NM 87504-2321 / USA
(505) 988-4418

Dedication

This book is dedicated to my children Jeffrey and Kristin, and grandchildren Olivia Thomas, Mary, and Jasmine.

Drawing made by Granddaughter.

CONTENTS

Introduction ~ 9

1. Fallen Leaves ~ 13
   Whereby the Leaves Have Fallen ~ 15

2. Sprouting Leaves ~ 19
   Historic Victorian Home ~26

3. Trouble in Paradise ~ 29

4. Little Acorns of Life ~ 33
   A Common Thread ~ 38

5. Sonoran Heritage Wheat ~ 51
   Prayer to St. Anthony for Our Children ~ 55

6. God's Hidden Hand ~ 61

7. Finding Hope and Peace ~69

8. Of Body and Blood ~ 73
   Saint Therese's Devotion to the Holy Face ~ 74
   A Call to a Deeper Love ~ 76

About the Author ~ 79

INTRODUCTION

As my spiritual journey progressed, I note the desire for material things lessened. Furthermore, over time I began to experience a near ever-presence of joy for by then I had determined what was most meaningful. These blessings were enhanced as a more humble nature emerged while I began to appreciate the smallest of things.

Whereby I exhibited blind faith and found that the more I did—the more the Holy Spirit revealed. Letting go and letting God direct my life was the turning point, for God opened all the doors I needed in order to fulfill my purpose in life. The joy and overwhelming peace I feel from the Holy Spirit's direction, not mine, is a grace available to anyone who prays for God's Holy Will.

I would have probably missed the opportunity to open the gift shop had it not been for St. Therese "the patroness of missions." Her novena promised to let a shower of roses fall from Heaven, while her hidden hand does good upon earth.

Thankfully, I came to recognize this gift from God and pray others will do the same, for it is amazing to see how it transforms one's life.

As a child, I marveled at the majestic world of the mystical mighty oak tree, whereby I dreamed of living amongst the swayed branches and whispering leaves of nature's canopy.

Many a day found myself lying in the shade of the mighty Oak while gazing at the Heavens above. I especially loved the times when the rustling of its leaves held whispers of my memories of the past. Meanwhile, acorns lined my pockets.

The adage of each leaf is a page in my journal of life which eventually falls to the woodland floor below. The trunk, so massive and strong, would surely be able to support my imaginary treehouse. The bark would protect me for I would then be safe and free. If I should climb the magical Oaktree, I could have a greater visual of the mountains above and watch the eagles soar to great heights.

Meanwhile, I would protect the little birds while they slept, then awaken at daybreak to join them in harmony, chirping praises to God, the creator, and His Son (sun). I could look down and feast my eyes on the fields of flowers carpeting the quiet wooded area below. I felt God would surely love this unique little soul even if the world failed to perceive it. For by continuing to reach for the summit of the mountain of love, I feel gentle and more confident, having more compassion and mercy for others. I shall follow God's perfect will for this little soul and thus become the beautiful flower I was meant to be.

Love,
Barbara Hegger-Romero.

Dearest Jesus,

I am only a single pink rose in your garden of Divine Love.
Please shower me with all the graces needed to work for the Glory of God.
Please help me to pluck the weeds of iniquity and sow the seeds of your Divine Mercy and Love.
Please help me to cultivate souls so they may someday see Your Holy Face in the Heavenly Garden
    of Your Angels and Saints.
Pluck the lilies of purity, Your Priest Sons, to kneel at Your Banquet Table.
Please Saint Therese guide me on the path of your little way, holding the hand of the little child,
    Jesus, while sowing the seeds of wisdom and perfect love.
Beckon the birds of your refuge, dropping seeds of vocations for your Heavenly Banquet...

—Barbara Hegger

1~ FALLEN LEAVES

The ancestral roots on my mother's fraternal side of our family tree originated in Baden Germany; arriving in America via New Orleans, subsequently forging down the mighty Mississippi to St. Louis, and eventually on to the fertile farmland of Illinois. Immigration in those days had to follow the laws of the kings and for the most part, individuals entered the country legally. Earlier in the 1800s, her great grandmother Barbara, who was originally from Lucerne, Switzerland traveled by ship from France to America—also arriving in New Orleans.

After which they went on to St. Louis and Illinois. Her family were Oak barrel makers and had come to the U.S. to escape religious persecution.

Eventually, my great-great-grandparents joined in the union of Holy Matrimony with my mother's grandfather, Joseph, who later became a trustee of the First National Bank of Highland. He subsequently invested in the company known as "Helvetia Milk Condensing Company" which in later years became the famous Pet Milk Company that was known all over the world.

I remember my grandfather talking about the stock he had in Pet Milk. During World War I, the servicemen called the milk can the tin cow. An immigrant from Switzerland brought to Highland, which was called Helvetia in the 1800s, a revolutionary process for canning milk as a substitute for fresh milk, where there was little refrigeration, and as wholesome, safe baby food, called condensed milk. The Helvetia company packaged the condensed milk in baby-sized cans nicknamed by the employees as pet milk, and that is how the "Pet" brand originated, thus Helvetia was renamed Pet.

In the midst of the Great Depression, Pet Milk became an important staple for American families. Pet helped supply Teddy Roosevelt's Rough Riders and other American fighting troops with a safe and convenient source of milk. Pet also supplied the U.S. troops fighting overseas in World War I as well as the GIs in World War Two. Thus, it all started in the town where I was born, Highland, Illinois.

There is an old family story that Joseph shared with his son, my grandfather, that there was land to be claimed in Oklahoma. Therefore, my grandfather and his friends went by horseback to claim acres of land in Oklahoma. Years later, oil wells were drilled on the land, and royalties for the family of seven were divided equally since his six sisters were always included in all of his investments.

As I recall, my grandfather had a beautiful smile and a twinkle in his eye. Furthermore, he was very generous with those in need and thus was highly respected by those in the community. His devotion to the Catholic Church was realized by his participation in the foundation of the "Shrine of Our Lady of the Snows" in Belleville, Illinois, and his memberships in the Holy Name Society, and the Knights of Columbus. He and several of his sisters donated vast amounts of money to the shrine, therefore their names are entered in bronze on the outdoor chapel walls.

One of his other sisters was married to the founder of the Wicks Organ Company which originally was the Wicks Brother's Jewelry and Watchmaking Store. It was in the same building as the Helvetia Milk Condensing Company, later known as the Pet Milk Company. The local Catholic priest asked John Wick to study organ and so he attended the university in St. Louis to learn music and organ; thereby using his talents as a watchmaker, cabinet maker, and jeweler.

He and his other two brothers founded the famous Wicks Organ Company, which still operates in the small town of Highland, Illinois. My great aunt was married to him and after their passing, I was given their wedding rosary.

My grandfather and two of his other sisters also contributed substantial amounts of money to the famous "Shrine of Our Lady of the Snows" in Illinois, which was molded after the Basilica of St. Mary Major in Rome. It was dedicated to the famous "Miracle of Our Lady of the Snows" as was the high school I graduated from, that being "Mater Dei High School," which means mother of God. The Tuition was free and students were taught by priests and nuns.

For as long as I can remember, I had a great devotion to the Blessed Mother. I always went to her when I experienced my trials and tribulations. My great aunts knew of my devotion to her. They had similar devotions to the Blessed Virgin and the Saints. A beautiful nursing home wing was built by and donated to the hospital by my two aunts where they subsequently lived out their final years.

My great aunts were also proud of their niece, Stella, and her achievements, having graduated at the top of her class and that too with honors, which was written up in the newspaper. Therefore, the later disappointment of her becoming pregnant devastated them greatly.

Great emphasis was placed on the bonds of marriage; those that deviated from this social norm faced condemnation from their community and peers. The future mother was stigmatized and the family was scandalized. Stella's mother had no say, for wives in those days rarely opposed, if ever, decisions made by their husbands.

The father of the child would have to be protected for he was a doctor and was looking to advance in his practice; he did not need this scandal in his life, for his family, like Stella's, were also very devout Catholics and very much connected to the church. Everyone had decided on the future of the baby except the victim who only wanted to take the responsibility of raising her child to no avail. The decision was made by others and her fate was sealed.

Whereby the Leaves Have Fallen

It was the summer of 1969. As I recall, the day was warm and sunny, therefore my husband and I, and a few of our friends were excited about spending the day on the river. Making it extra special was the fact that such outings were rare, as my husband oftentimes worked long hours and I was busy tending to our baby. Also having grown up on a farm in Illinois, I always cherished time spent outdoors, even if it included my siblings and me having to lend a hand with the chores. As I remember, I felt free, as a gentle breeze rustled my hair while I was being bathed in sunlight. I also remember having admired my reflection in the shadows. Then I always felt great when I wore my favorite pink ruffled crop top, furthermore, I was pleased as I was quick to regain my figure following the recent birth of our son. I was on the dock watching the men tie our boats together with ropes. At the time, it seemed like a great idea...

Although the decision would soon prove to have been otherwise. The men helped us onto the boats and it wasn't long before we were on our way down the river.

Unfortunately, our boat hit a huge tree trunk that was protruding out of the water.

Consequently, the boats flipped over, and we all fell into the water, which now appeared murky. I tried to swim away from underneath the capsized boat, but the current kept pulling me back. The fear I felt, knowing I may never hold my infant son again devastated me. Furthermore, I wasn't certain if my husband had survived the accident. In the midst of my terror, I wondered if I would fulfill my mission in life when suddenly I was pulled from the water by a stranger, a woman who later said she was a nurse. She said she had seen the pink straps upon the water and realized someone was trapped beneath the boat, whereby she acted quickly. As my journey progressed, I eventually noted there were other instances in which angels may have appeared.

As fate would have it, the rather haunting near-drowning experience caused me to think of what my Aunt Stella had to have endured. While screaming for her baby, who had been taken away, her eyes never to behold his gaze, never to sing him lullabies, while cradling him in her loving arms.

As I recall, my aunt Stella was both brilliant and beautiful. She graduated as a registered nurse with high honors rated at the top of her class. Her flaxen gold hair was smooth as silk. Her blue eyes were filled with light. Her voice was melodious, a reflection of her joy.

After graduating from the School of Nursing in Ashland Wisconsin in October of 1941, she qualified to receive Reciprocity; the title of a Registered Nurse licensed in the State of Missouri, in June of 1943. She subsequently met a future doctor who was doing his internship at nearby hospitals and later had his office near where she lived; with my parents in South St. Louis.

Apparently, there was immediate chemistry between them, therefore it was not long before they became intimate through which they say she had fallen hopelessly in love and was imagining their future together. Although, her having given in to temptation, ultimately led to pain and tragedy.

When she announced she was pregnant with his child, her lover rejected her. Her feeling of abandonment and shame was intensified by the fact that her three married sisters were having babies that year. The physician who had fathered her child then married another, two months before the arrival of Stella and his baby. Not only did her dreams crumble when he rejected her, but his marriage to some other woman broke her heart.

Furthermore, her future of raising her baby would never be. The circumstances surrounding the incident took a good while to come to light; for much was shrouded in secrecy or else buried amidst the "fallen leaves of our family tree." The decision of others to put the episode behind them did not make the memory go away. Therefore, the relationships of the siblings changed, and much would be concealed that transpired with the passage of time and likened to the changing colors of the fallen leaves—whereby hope would ultimately rise again when individuals married and had children.

In the interim, some unions failed due to the pressures of the world—while others thrived. Therefore, I knew faith was an ever- essential ingredient of a joyful and purposeful life and the more I embraced that belief, the more magical things became, for it felt as though angels were near.

Due to the sensitivity I had to her plight, I would eventually uncover what had shaken our family's core. Early on, I realized the importance of forgiveness; I also became aware of the difficulties that can arise when we harbor hatred or perhaps fail to seek forgiveness for our own misdeeds as well as to grant forgiveness to others.

Some years later, my father informed my younger sister and me that he had been appointed to take my aunt to the hospital to have the baby. At the time Stella lived with them, he was present during the birth and witnessed Stella's screams for her baby, while the baby was being taken away immediately after his birth. She was not allowed to even see or hold her newborn.

Therefore, the tiny infant entered the world never knowing his mother's touch. Our father claimed he was under pressure to sign some papers, something he regrets to this day.

Before this tragedy, my mother's parents had been pillars of the community, devout Catholics, who were active in the church, although having been shamed by the unwed daughter's pregnancy, their appearances at social functions lessened. The rumors ran rampant as to why the young doctor had abandoned her—others may have wondered if she had hoped to ensnare her lover and so on, for much goes on in the minds of people when mystery surrounds us.

Sadly, our father became another victim of the tragedy. My mother pleaded with my father to have Stella and her baby live with them, but he refused. He maintained it was too late, for the pre-arranged deal had already been implemented. Since my father was sworn to secrecy about the future of the child, only he and my grandfather knew the family secret. My father later claimed this event created the rift in their marriage that subsequently led to their divorce years later. When my father visited me in Los Luceros in New Mexico about ten years ago, he told me that my mother had never wanted me, which I found a very strange thing to say to your daughter and I always wondered why she did not want me for I had done nothing to her to warrant her hatred towards me.

Having always been sensitive to what oftentimes was an unseen presence, eventually, the many pieces of the puzzle began coming together. Our mother informed my younger sister and me that she and Stella felt the baby lived nearby, therefore the radius of my search narrowed. Meanwhile my grandmother Rose was affected deeply, and never was the same again. As fate would have it, our mother was the only family member that visited Stella for the others chose to put the unpleasant incident behind them and move on with their lives.

Through my persistent search, many truths were revealed to me. Placement of the baby with a loving family was always in my thoughts for I knew that baby was not put in an orphanage. Fact is, my grandfather confided in the local priest and he suggested perhaps a family wanting a boy that was a distant relative. You see, everything was done beneath the falling leaves of the family tree.

Headlines: August 19, 1969

"Prominent physician, his wife, and their son were swept off the pier by eight-foot waves. The physician saved his son and then went back into the choppy waters to save his wife. She was rescued by others a short while later. The breakers were swift and the coast guard lost sight of him, they recovered his body the next morning. Ironically, he had rescued his adopted son—but in the end, death dealt the final blow, as they were separated."

I wondered if this could be the physician that fathered my long-lost cousin? I then recalled that this was the same month and year that I nearly drowned, the raging river pinning me under the boat, realizing I may never be able to hold my infant son again and experiencing the miracle of the angel who had saved me; for my mission on earth has yet to be completed...

Even to this day, the identity of my aunt Stella's baby has never been revealed. Or perhaps you can say it still remains a mystery.

2 ~ SPROUTING LEAVES

As a child growing up in a large family of seven children, I have fond memories of my parents cramming us all into a maroon Studebaker, headed for Sunday mass, while we were attired in our frilly Easter dresses, flowery straw bonnets, little white gloves, and black patent leather shoes. My two brothers donned their Sunday best suits, crisp white shirts, and ties. As always, we were excited to come home to our Easter baskets filled with chocolate bunnies, jelly beans, and eggs of all colors. We hid the eggs so many times that they were beyond being edible.

We were always greeted after school by our mother, with scrumptious cinnamon rolls and freshly baked bread… I can still recall a time when my mother made me feel special when she sewed me a beautiful sundress made of a flowing, floral, fabric that was identical to hers. Oddly enough, my mother never said the words, I love you, perhaps she had grown up in an environment in which such demonstration of affection was rarely expressed.

As a child, I loved to venture off into the woods behind our house and bathe in the beauty of the stillness before me, and how the mighty oaks towered above me, offering their branches, and leaves of many colors for my viewing; handfuls of acorns lay before me for my taking, which I remember taking home to keep near me. I clearly remember that the wildflowers blanketed the field with many colors and varieties, I wondered how tiny seeds could fill a field with flowers.

Peace and tranquility filled my soul in those hours.

My summers were filled with adventure, for reading sixty books a summer to me was an adventure into the lives of saints, especially the little flower St. Therese of the Child Jesus and the Holy Face. I ventured alone to a daily mass, which was something my mother could not help but notice and silently admired; for when I was older, she told me that I was the only one of her children that attended mass faithfully. She may have liked my need for faith similar to her own—my mother's lack of maternal expressions of love was made up for in other ways.

My school days were filled with events of cheerleading, school plays which I received best supporting actress for, shortstop position for our softball team, and winning awards for board jump and hurdles.

One of the hurdles in my life was getting over my mistrust of others' intentions. I was taught always to be honest and to always tell the truth no matter what, which ended up getting me in trouble with others; I call them little acorns in my life (lessons). We were also taught to be seen and not be heard; so, I saw that my oldest sister was treated differently than the rest of us, but I was never allowed to question this. She was the only one allowed to take private music lessons, the only one to be shared in the family secrets; she was regarded as having a higher place in heaven, according to my mother, because she was going to the convent to become a nun.

Later, she left the convent and married a priest; so, innocently, I asked my mother if she had lost her high place in heaven, only to get a slap across the face for questioning the situation.

Another incident that crosses my mind; was when the cows broke out of the fence and we all had to round them up to the barn. My mother told me to run to the barn and open the door; when I got to the barn the only closed door was the one in the back, so I opened the door, not to question anybody; the cows were herded in through the front door and out the back to the other field—later, my mother told me to check the electric fence, to see if it was on, not to question it, I went to check and received a bolt of electricity, and thus proclaimed that it was on. This may be why I have been cautious of others.

Further along in my life, my mother had called me one day, to let me know that she was going to the hospital the next morning for minor surgery. The next day I did my routine errands, and as I was leaving the bank, on the sidewalk were pennies strewn in a number by my feet. I right away thought of my mother and how she stressed to pick up a penny for good luck. I even giggled to myself that she was somehow a part of this.

That same evening, my oldest sister called and said our mother was on life support and may not make it. I was devastated, how could this be, she was an avid walker, and very healthy—then I got the news that she had passed away. The plane ride to her funeral was full of conflict and pain, for I did not get to tell her goodbye.

In the wake, I could not bring myself to come up to see her in the coffin but my sisters encouraged me to do so. I stood before her and quietly asked her why she never said those words to me, "I love you."

Some months later, a dear priest at my parish invited those that had recently lost loved ones to bring to church a picture so they would be prayed for on all soul's day. I brought along a lovely picture of my mother, set it on the table with the other ones there, and went quietly back to my seat, only to notice a shiny penny laying at my feet. I picked up the penny, turned it over, and to my amazement, saw a heart burnt into the penny. I later confided in the parish priest about my mother and the penny; he agreed with me that this was the way my mother answered my question at the wake to tell me she loved me. Instantly, I was healed of my pain, instantly I experienced total forgiveness of her—As St. Therese says—God shows love by mercy and forgiveness.

I have fond childhood memories of my father as well; having told me about the oak trees in the woods behind our home that produced the acorns I always loved to gather. Therefore, at an early age, I became intrigued by the mystery the acorn held, which would eventually give rise to the mighty oak. He explained how every spring the oak trees would bloom and that as the leaves unfolded, yellow pollen fell to the ground thereby signaling it is almost time for the two of us to go morel mushroom hunting.

Although he added, it took a heavy rain, and a few days of sunshine to warm the ground before the mushrooms would appear, after which we grabbed some gunny sacks and ventured out to the woods to our secret hiding place where the mushrooms were hiding under the fallen elm leaves. This truly was a gift of the spring wood's natural environment, offering us vitamin-rich food for our taking. Even the banks of the creek that ran through the middle of the woods offered us more of the nutty-tasting morels—that we all loved to feast on.

We would cut off the mushrooms near the bottom of the stem and fill our gunnysacks to take home for my mother to fix for the family dinner. My mother would carefully clean each one, and then sauté them in butter. As I recall, the warm, fragrant aroma would fill the room. She also made creamed mushrooms, which were my favorite, for the nutty flavor tantalized my taste buds…

Rather early on, my father nicknamed me Bobbi, which stuck with me through my young adult life and then some. After I graduated from high school, I went to live with my father. Being that my parents had separated a few months earlier and he was the one who had shown me affection, I went to live with him.

Once I settled in, my father secured employment for me at his friend's Greek restaurant. I wanted to do well and make my father proud of me, so I was adamant about doing everything by the book, in this case by the menu. My very first customer ordered one egg, toast, and coffee—which I explained to him was not on the menu; now we had two eggs, but not one egg. His look of disdain told me he was not happy. He angrily ordered the two eggs.

As I set his order on the table, he grabbed a knife and cut one of the eggs off the plate and threw it on the floor, after which he exclaimed, "Now that's one egg." Needless to say, he was charged for two, since the register was set up that way, and I had to ring the bill up right.

My father, a manager at Sears, which was next door, along with his fellow workers would frequent the restaurant for lunch, and ask for my table. He was delighted by my story of "going by the menu," whereby we all laughed about it and became very close.

One day, my father announced to them that his daughter, Bobbi, was getting married. When and why; so, I told them that I had to get married because I had too many morals and I could never live with my boyfriend. You could see the relieved look on all their faces...

After I got married, I worked in an exclusive upscale restaurant where they served alcohol, which was another learning experience, since my parents never consumed alcohol. Therefore, I never knew anything about liquor or fancy drinks. I was assigned to take drink orders for an elite party of businessmen, where a gentleman ordered anisette; so, I obliged and brought him an Anacin with a glass of water. His look of utter disbelief told me he did not have a headache and I better be on my way to get him his after-dinner liquor...

My father, through the years, was a rather good sport about things. He had a welcoming smile for me and others. I will never forget the time when Christmas arrived, and I had no gifts for him; our newborn daughter was just a few weeks old, and my husband did not take me Christmas shopping; so, I waited for him to come home from work, figuring he may have gotten a Christmas gift from a girlfriend. I went to his car, opened the trunk, and sure enough, there in front of me was an unwrapped gift which included a shirt, tie, and hat.

What luck, I rewrapped his gift and took it to my father's. I laid it under the tree with the rest of the presents. The look on my husband's face was precious, for he knew what I had done. My father opened his gifts and thanked my husband and me for the shirt, tie, and lovely hat. At times like this, my reward was bitter-sweet.

Like most fathers, my father was good for advice—at times. He was especially helpful through my marital problems and my husband's infidelities. He told me the reason my husband was accusing me of things was because he was doing the very thing that he was accusing me of. In a bid to save the marriage, I even went so far as to get counseling. Then I thought I must be doing something wrong for my husband to be so cruel to me. According to him, I did not talk right nor look right. Although, the counselor assured me there was nothing wrong with me, and said that there was something wrong with him.

After a while, I filed for divorce.

Moreover, I left him with everything and took our daughter with me to Texas. I was hoping to find a new life there and secure a position in the airline industry. My son, on the other hand, did not want to leave his father, thus granting him his wishes, he stayed with his father.

Before having set out for Houston, we packed our suitcases and gathered all of my daughter's toys, the favorite of which was her Cabbage Patch Doll. The joy she derived from it more than made up for the hours I stood in line with hordes of other parents, who like myself, were willing to do whatever it took to make their little girl's Christmas wish come true. The sacrifice I made was well worth it, for my daughter's imaginary playmate sat next to her as we headed towards our new life that I prayed was awaiting us. Understandably, I had a heavy heart due to a failed marriage, plus having to leave my son behind.

Although I leaned upon God more than ever, whereby I felt near my son despite the distance. Soon after the divorce, our daughter and I drove to Houston, where I answered a newspaper ad for a security position at the Intercontinental Airport. I was called and I made an appointment with a woman named Marty, that was to be held at the security office in a hotel on the grounds of the airport.

The next morning, I drove to the hotel and walked in through the front entrance not knowing whether to go to the left or the right, so, I felt inclined to go right. As I walked into the office, a friendly, petite blonde woman was sitting at her desk in front of a computer, whereby she turned to me and asked me if she could help me. I was not certain if I was in the right place, so I told her I had an interview with a lady named Marty. I noted she had a surprised look on her face, as she informed me her name was Marty.

She told me no one from the main office had mentioned any interview, but she could use an assistant manager. She then went on to add that her company blocked seats from Pan Am, for military flights, and eventually she would teach me the saber system (if I got the job). She then sent me on my way and said she would call me in a few days to let me know if I got the job.

Sure enough, two days later she called me and had me come in for another interview.

While she was asking me personal questions, we discovered that we were both born the same day, and month, and had been married to men that were born the same day, and month. The business relationship developed into a wonderful friend relationship as well.

Both my daughter and I ended up finding a great friend in Marty.

Eventually, the job took me to the place I wanted to be; working as a gate agent, ticket agent, and customer service rep. for Texas International, which later became Continental Airlines. I was later appointed Passenger Service Rep. which required numerous airport duties; from coordinating the ticket counter with the gates, to boarding announcements, to handling passengers with all flight-related issues.

One time, they needed someone on the tarmac to direct a flight to the gate. I was very happy in my position since I could prevent passengers from missing flights due to long lines and they would be ever so grateful. But when there are layoffs, you adapt and take whatever position you can. I took a reservation job there near the Houston Intercontinental Airport and learned another side of the airline business.

Barbara in Chicago in 1982 when employed by Continental Airlines.

After a while, I decided to move to the Chicago Reservation Center, in order to be closer to my family. My daughter and I enjoyed our time together and loved flying to various cities in the United States while taking in the beauty of the different landscapes that our country has to offer.

I remember buying her a bright floral pattern Hawaiian Muumuu, which she wore with orchid leis. Her beautiful, long, black hair complimented her outfit, while her eyes reflected her delight. She wore it to Bobby McGee's Restaurant, where an Elvis Presley impersonator called her on stage so he could sing Blue Hawaii to her. The incident made her feel so special. She was very precious to me. I recall how her name was given to me when I was in my eighth month of carrying her. I had the name Jill picked out, but for whatever reason, the name Kristin Joy came to me out of the blue; that backward is Joy- in-Krist (read: Joy-in-Christ).

Unlike my mother, I showered my children with affection. My mother and I were also different in the way that she was home when we were children, while my children had to experience a working mother, who was always trying to keep them taken care of financially. I so regretted being away from them, therefore I understand why my daughter wanted to be a stay-at-home mother.

Eventually, my ex-husband and I got back together, he let me know he was wrong and that he had been immature, but now he had changed, and he was ready to be a loving husband and father. So, we remarried and it took less than one year before he was unfaithful again.

Historic Victorian Home

Original Victorian Home.

What is now a historic Victorian home in Avison, Illinois by the railroad depot, was purchased by my grandfather, a local barber. My father Everest was the first of his ten siblings to be born there, marking the beginning of the invisible thread that appears to have been part of some divine tapestry.

My grandmother, Anna, an avid gardener, took much pride in her prize-winning rose bushes. My father would snip a few roses and give them to some girls in town.

(From left to right): Godfather (Charlie), Grandmother (Anna) and Father (Everest).

I have fond memories as a toddler of the small village in Aviston, Illinois where my grandfather, William Hegger, a local barber, purchased the architectural piece in 1920.

Aviston was a bustling railroad hub in those days and subsequently my grandmother made sure the hobos from the train were not on their way until she gave them a good meal. A mark was left on the iron gate to alert others of the good home cooked meal they could have here on the porch.

As a child, I remember the house as being unique with a massive staircase that led to the upstairs landing. It had a decorative fireplace with a cast iron cover, and huge pocket doors that led to the parlor. A wooden plate shelf lined the dining room wall. The round turret was where my grandfather's roll top desk stayed.

My grandmother, Anna, was known for her kindness and compassion for others. She took great pride in her lovely roses. My father's sister, Anna Mae, and my uncle, Marvin, shared the story of my godfather Charles' incident of the lost glasses. He was with him at Carson City Casino when Charlie misplaced his glasses and left word with security, giving his name and address.

Soon, a man came up to him and asked him about Aviston, Illinois. I have been through there on occasion. *I remember the meals I had on the porch of the residence next to the railroad tracks. The gate was marked as a place where one could get a hearty meal.* Charlie acknowledged that the kind woman, an excellent cook, was indeed his mother. Well, I am the one who found your glasses. Just so you know, I was one of those hobos.

3 ~ TROUBLE IN PARADISE

Soon after I had transferred with my job at the airlines to the Continental Reservation Center in Chicago, my daughter and I began hearing regularly from her father. His job with General Electric often took him to meetings at their corporate office in Chicago. Whenever he was in town he would come and visit with his daughter Kristin. It wasn't long before he took the family out to dinner, bringing gifts, after which due to the sense of family that I had longed for, the relationship blossomed, therefore my subsequent decision to marry again felt like a dream come true as I had missed my son terribly while I was away.

The renewed feelings of closeness as a family came back and he convinced me that he was a changed man and wanted us back again as a family. In my heart, I wanted to believe him, for I had forgiven of all his wrongdoings, yet I also knew that it was hard to forget.

After a few months, I decided to leave my job. I was happy and excited about being a family again. We attended baseball games where my son was the pitcher, where he played varsity as a sophomore; and football, where he was the kicker.

We bought a charming house across the street from our children's high school which was convenient for both our children to participate fully in their activities. Our daughter was in the queen's court for homecoming and excelled in swimming and track. She also did well in school, receiving a full-ride scholarship to a college near Chicago.

The children were encouraged by their father to excel in sports, for he played on three baseball teams and wanted them to have the same love for sports that he had. In high school, I also enjoyed playing softball and jumping hurdles and broad jumps. But our parents had also instilled hard work and we wanted our children to one day be independent and achieve what they wanted by working for it. So, my son started out with a paper route and when he was sick, I would be out there at five in the morning, rain or shine or snow, the delivering newspapers.

One morning, I must not have been fully awake, because I forgot to put the car in park and proceeded to open the door to get out of the car. The moving vehicle caused me to fall to the ground. I watched the wheels pass my eyes as I lay there for a while; realizing the car was moving and I needed to stop it before it hit a house at the end of the block. I struggled to get up because I had hurt my leg in the fall and started running with a painful limp down the street after my car. I jumped in the crawling car just in time to put the brake and stop the car. I remembered the Guardian Angel's Prayer that I used to recite every night. "Angel of God, my Guardian dear to whom His love commits me here; if I die before I wake, I pray the Lord puts on the brake"!

I still went to work that day at a nearby store and my manager wanted to know what happened. I, of course, told him the truth, only to find out that "Bobbi almost running over herself" was the opening statement the manager made at the morning store meeting. Just like the time I fell over a cart of merchandise that was not in my view while I was on the phone selling a customer product, all done as I lay on the floor, hurt from the fall. But as the manager said, "She still got the sale."

I always hated leaving my children while going off to work, but they wanted the name-brand clothes, the expensive Nike and Jordan shoes, and a car like their friends. My husband told me that I would have to work full time in order to send my son to college in the future, for Drake University was where he wanted to go. So, we do all of these things for our children, wanting them to have what we did not have as children, and making it easier for them so they would not have to go through the financial difficulties that we had.

I also worked at the local radio station part-time; announcing the news and weather, and having my own program of music for which I created a theme, dedicating the old songs from Mexico and the Hispanics.

People would call in and praise my choice of music which I got in trouble for because according to the manager, "I was changing their format." I had a few favorite tunes that I played often, "Lady in Red" and "Don't Cry for me Argentina."

Soon, the annual Band Festival was approaching and I was asked to be on the KCMR float and represent with other employees, a famous Gothic Painting. We were not allowed to even crack a smile while in the parade, which was hard to do as the crowd was trying to get us to smile. We ended up getting the second-place trophy for that year.

Many people came because of the significance of Mason City as being the boyhood home of Meredith Willson, who wrote the famous classic musical, "The Music Man" with actress Shirley Jones (Marion, the Librarian), filmed in River City (Mason City). Many marching bands from all over the state descended upon the town in all their festive uniforms, signaling the school they were from.

In recent years, the Music Man Museum opened to show the history of the grand celebration. Those were some joyous times. But not all shared, for my husband was away on business, a lot. At first, my husband was attentive and he would take me at times to the business events, but I loved to dance so he would take me to the annual Buddy Holly Winter Dance Party at the Surf Ballroom which was a few miles from where we lived.

Everyone used to dress in the 1950s style, many girls were attired with poodle skirts and bobby sox with tennis shoes. While the guys wore Levis, leather jackets, and converse high tops with some saddle shoes. They rolled up their t-shirts and held their cigarette packs to be cool. Buddy Holly had died in a plane crash in the Clear Lake and the tribute to him included the clothes worn in that period of time. Those times were far and few between, for my husband's job had him traveling a good deal; where he had the opportunity to meet other women—still I sensed amidst his infidelities that there was a desire for a sense of family.

I always had hope that things had changed but in reality, it had only gotten worse. I found myself in the comfort of friends, finding peace in my faith, going to church more, and reading St. Therese's favorite little book by Thomas á Kempis, the *Imitation of Christ*. The Bible readings and prayers gave me hope that this second marriage with my husband would succeed this time. I chose to ignore the things that bothered me, while merely hoping our relationship would improve. I wanted to shield my children from the pain of having perhaps to have to go through another divorce. But with time, I noticed my husband communicating less as oftentimes he was away on work. Not wanting to hurt my children, and not wanting to disappoint my parents again, all I could do was hope.

Time revealed my suspicions, the truth once again came to light when I paid an unexpected visit to my husband when he was in the hospital, awaiting a new heart for transplant surgery. I approached his bed and noticed a note had been left for him. He was away with orderlies at the time of my discovery so I read the note which was clearly visible and not in an envelope—my first reaction was that it might be for a nurse or even for me.

The note was from his ongoing affair with his lover and she wanted to know when it was safe and clear for her to visit him. This discovery made me snap and I realized that he was living a double life for some time now and was emotionally invested in her and her children's lives. I decided to stay with him through the surgery, after which. about a year later, we parted ways.

Many years later, the guilt he felt was no longer silent—for he called me only months before his passing and sought my forgiveness, which I quickly granted him, not knowing he was in his final days. He died between his children's birthdays, on the 10th of December, and was buried on his son's birthday. I was grateful to God that he granted us this opportunity to forgive each other.

His family never kept in contact with me after that; however, a few years back my son told me that his aunt, his dad's sister was in a coma from a fall. The doctors felt there was no hope, but her children would not give up and refused to take her off life support. I sent my card of the single pink rose with St. Anthony's to her family, expressing my concern and prayers for her complete recovery. My son was also praying for her. He called me some months later to let me know that she had regained a full recovery and was nearly back to where she was before the fall. My son's heartfelt prayers for her were always sincere and I have always had hope in God's will for us and know that he has us in the palm of his hands.

4 ~ LITTLE ACORNS OF LIFE

Through my little acorns (life's lessons), I grew much in my faith. As a child, I excelled in religion and history, I loved attending mass and being alone with Jesus. My love for books earned me certificates for the most books read in a summer. I especially liked the story of Saint Therese the Little Flower. Later in life, I met a nurse who shared my spirituality. Together, we were on Saint Therese's path of Love and Forgiveness.

She said that love knows how to make the best of everything, for true charity consists of bearing all things including the defects in others. We are to accept with gratitude, the thorns mixed with the flowers. Prayer is an aspiration of the heart, it is a simple glance directed to heaven, it is a cry of gratitude and love in the midst of trial as well as joy. Finally, it is something great, and supernatural, which expands my soul and unites me to Jesus.

I soon realized that Saint Therese's favorite reading was the *Imitation of Christ* by Thomas á Kempis, which was also my favorite book.

My friend and I were hooked, as we traveled many miles away to the Carmelite Monastery, to view Saint Therese's reliquary, and pray for her intersession, by asking for a sign from her of a single pink rose, since she was known for it, and before she died, she said, "I will let fall from Heaven... a shower of roses." St. Therese spent Heaven doing good on earth.

Prior to our travel to a symposium, my friend and I prayed a novena to St. Therese, and as a sign from my friend, a dozen red roses, and a single pink rose from me. The cathedral where we attended mass, was very majestic and had bouquets of red and white roses.

My friend remarked that there were no pink roses, but I felt I did not need a sign for my faith was always strong. As I looked to my right, I saw a niche with St. Joseph's statue, surrounded by vases of red and white roses. I wanted to pray there, so after mass, my friend and I made our way up to the front of the church and we knelt to pray before St. Joseph. Suddenly, one of the white roses turned a solid pink.

St. Therese had delivered the single pink rose that I was promised. The scent of roses permeated the air at different times, letting us know these happenings were from Heaven. There have been other Heavenly happenings throughout my life. St. Therese says that suffering itself becomes the greatest of joys when we seek it as a precious treasure.

I recall the time I was airlifted to the hospital near death for mistakenly drinking a high percentage of hydrogen peroxide. My daughter called the ambulance and they took me to the local hospital, after which I had to be airlifted to a hospital that had a hyperbaric chamber since I had lost all muscle control.

Hours later, my faithful friends rushed to the hospital to come to my aid and pray for me. I noticed that a picture with the novena to St. Therese was placed under my pillow. Oddly enough, the nurse in my room was dressed unlike the others and she attended to me where her presence gave me peace.

Early the next morning they came to take me to the hyperbaric chamber when they realized I had come out of the condition and had no need to be placed in there. The doctors were amazed at my recovery.

As I recall, it was a beautiful summer day and I was enjoying driving through the countryside of rural Iowa while heading for a tiny Irish village called Dougherty. I was so looking forward to a visit with my precious friends, all of whom are residing at the convent of the "Sisters of the Presentation of the Blessed Virgin Mary," that is located on Patrick Street.

As I drove around the unfamiliar areas of the rural landscape, I was praying I was on the right road when I noticed a sign that read "A little bit of Ireland and they call it Dougherty," population fifty-six. I figured it should not be too difficult to find the convent and St. Patrick's Church.

Incidentally, it was at the end of the mile-long main street. Dougherty is the type of town one can buy flowers and other incidentals and purchase tires all at the same place. Although they do have a tiny post office that was built in 1890, it had only one employee who was 92 years old and she has likely been there since it opened, she also has the key to open the bank whenever you called to complete a transaction for whatever it may be. It was clearly reminiscent of a bygone era for all is done by hand and computers were not utilized, nor had they been invented. I could not help but notice the main street didn't have sidewalks.

Thereby I instantly knew I had opened a new chapter in my life.

When I arrived, the sisters as always were delightful and full of joy as they welcomed me. A wonderful lunch had been prepared specially and was awaiting my arrival.

Vegetables from their garden, fresh-baked bread, homemade jams, as well as Irish potatoes were all part of the feast.

As might be expected, they were excited to show me their tiny chapel which I noted was very traditional and had recently been renovated by Father Ricardo whom I had yet to meet and who the sisters spoke of fondly. The sisters were pleased noting that now the chapel had added an old-world flavor. During the father's three-year stay, he designed and created stained glass windows, one for each year presently graced by the chapel. They then asked if I could spend the night whereby, I could attend mass in the early morning hours.

Following mass, we had breakfast at which time Father Ricardo and I were introduced to one another where I then would discover a gentle, holy priest who was born in Guadalajara and had moved here temporarily from Madrid, Spain.

Within days, I rented the cottage, and Father and I became neighbors. In the months that followed, a friendship developed between Father and me for he had many of the attributes I had always admired. Over time, I learned that he had worked with Father Amorith who had been involved with exorcisms. I was especially moved by Father's dedication to saving souls.

Another discovery, as it relates to Father Ricardo, occurred when he came to Chimayo in New Mexico to bless my store, imparting upon the endeavor that fate undoubtedly had led me to. The grand opening of my gift shop coincided with Easter, the very time when 60,000 would descend upon the area as a pilgrimage to Our Lord. I was still feeling the afterglow of the occasion when Father Ricardo arrived weeks later to officially bless my gift shop. He immediately noticed a collection of saint statues that I had purchased for the shop.

Due to the overwhelming preparations for the opening, I had little time to identify each and every saint in the collection.

Being a person with a great presence who appeared to prefer solitude, I sensed that he was intrigued by one of the statues. I was surprised when he asked me where I had gotten this statue and if I knew who it represented... I exclaimed I did not know who he was. He then told me that this saint was Saint Toribio from Mexico, who was his relative. Father went on to elaborate that St. Toribio was a martyr and shot in the Christero War in 1928. He went on to say that St. Toribio was canonized and became the patron of immigrants.

A number of years would pass before I would discover his interest as well as his involvement with the Shroud of Turin... In retrospect, I cannot dismiss the fact he had a devotion to St. Therese as a child. I knew St. Therese was involved for she always had ways of putting people together.

Looking back on my life, I realize how very blessed I had been with the friendships of the sisters and others. Also, when considering the number of instances in which St. Therese has made her presence known, I can't help but feel comfort and love. As always, one is humbled by the workings of the Holy Spirit. Also feeling blessed for the instances that are enabling me to explore the earlier interest of our beloved Saint Therese. Instances that have enabled me to explore our beloved saint's interest in the Holy Face and Shroud of Turin.

In the course of recounting my journey as well as paying tribute to a beloved saint;

having written what I have thus far while intending not only to recount my journeys as to pay tribute to Saint Therese. You feel you are lending credence to what others might dispel as happenstance.

The very fact that Father Ricardo and I met is a clear indication that there may be a bigger picture.

Furthermore, I marvel at the way the saints continue to have an influence in our lives when one merely believes.

As the year 2005 drew to a close, I reflected upon the losses of loved ones, my mother, as well as my brother who made his transition some six months later.

By the time 2006 rolled in. it appeared to do so with greater ease, for by them, I was beginning to sense the Holy Spirit might be guiding me. By that time, the faith I had embraced at an early age had deepened as I noted it had consistently sustained me in the times of trial whereby more and more joy would surround me. In following my instincts to this day, I have vivid memories and signs where I felt a shift to a more prayerful life. Oftentimes, I noted how in times of loss, disappointments, and pain, it brings one to a deeper understanding as we tend to lean on our Lord than having connected with what I perceive was my call.

Another element of what now appears to have been a part of a far greater picture fell into place a few days after Father Ricardo had blessed my gift shop when Glenda, a writer/screenwriter who I had mentioned earlier had occasion to visit.

As previously described, we connected seemingly instantly as she was interested in anything I might have that involved St. Therese. She stated that she had a close relationship with the Carmelite order and went on to ask. She was visiting New Mexico presently as she had accompanied a young friend who had recently moved to Santa Fe. In the course of our warm exchange, she mentioned she had spent several days in Durango, for not being a dessert person, she was longing to be near the water, whereby I told her about Los Luceros and the purely magical way I had come to live there.

Prior to her leaving the gift shop, we exchanged contact information, and having conversed several times, I asked her if she would like to visit me at my home in Los Luceros. She accepted and spent a few days enjoying the beauty and sounds of silence.

Consequently, I suddenly found myself living in a Historic Setting. I soon discovered the place was steeped in tales of well-known writers and artists, who like myself, had presumably enjoyed its beauty. Meanwhile, I felt a sense of what had preceded my arrival, as I enjoyed the warmth of the heart side or else the sounds of the nearby river. Once again, the sound of leaves rustling in the wind held memories of my childhood and my father and I gathering mushrooms. Being the place came with its own Capia, I recalled the many times I had attended mass on my very own while my mother commented on it. The recollections I had were often vivid, therefore it wasn't long before I realized how my faith had always seen me through even the roughest of times. Then there were countless instances in which St. Therese had interceded.

Far from where the acorns had gathered as a child fell, I discovered a connection to my father's family tree. It was while I was researching the history of Los Luceros that I began to read about the various individuals who over the years had stayed there.

Intrigued by the fact many were writers, I decided to delve into their lives a bit further. It was while I was researching the life of author Sinclair Lewis that I read where his wife Grace Livingston Hegger turned out to be related to my father.

As I further explored the amazing find of a relative who had been a fashion icon editor of Vogue Magazine, I couldn't help but notice an image of a poster announcing a Sinclair Exhibition. As I examined the poster more closely, I saw where it featured a movie marque that read "Rosebud Movie." I of course took the unexpected discovery as an affirmation that St. Therese had once again interceded in my life. Therefore, I was where I was presently.

If my hunch was right, it was not by chance that I ended up in New Mexico and subsequently owned a gift shop with religious art and artifacts that was across the way. Furthermore, the majority of my days were being spent next to a Historic Shrine where thousands gather annually to celebrate Christ's Resurrection. Adding to the intrigue of how it was all tied together was the fact in the course of my travels I had met and befriended a priest who for years had studied, as well as lectured on the Shroud of Turin.

I note the more I exhibited blind faith, the more the Holy Spirit would reveal His presence. Thereby the instances in which saints would intercede in my life was made known. In my having recounted my journey in the form of "Whereby the Leaves Have Fallen," it is my hope that others might recall similar instances in their lives through which their faith deepens.

A Common Thread

Los Luceros "Morning Star" lies within the heart of Northern New Mexico like a scene in a film full of mystery and intrigue. Therein lies the invincible thread that connected those who were destined to meet. Common threads of thinking and action all stitched together that simultaneously yet independently bound them forever in the common thread of living their dreams.

Many successful artists, writers, and photographers from around the world were welcomed by the owner, Mary Cabot Wheelwright, a Bostonian socialite whose mother was friends with Ralph Waldo Emerson. She had connections with the famous painter, Georgia O'Keeffe who frequently had luncheons with Mary in the dining room of the Casa Grande and High Tea with Georgia in Abiquiu. The two were well acquainted for they met years ago in New York City at social gatherings and art exhibitions.

Another wealthy patron of the arts from New York was Mabel Dodge Luhan who met Georgia O'Keeffe during her stay at her home on 5th Avernur New York City. She offered her a trip to Taos New Mexico, free lodging, and her own studio. Georgia O'Keeffe found this irresistible. Once she arrived, her life was never the same. She subsequently lived at the Kiowa ranch of the famous author D.H. Lawrence and painted the tree of ponderosa pine from the bench that Lawrence wrote his many novels. In fact, one of her favorite paintings is the "Lawrence Tree."

Another famous writer, Mary Hunter Austin, who often wrote from her oak treehouse, was among the cultural circle in Carmel, California. Mary Hunter Austin and Mabel Dodge Luhan became good friends and eventually moved to the Land of Enchantment.

Austin was active in preserving the local culture of New Mexico and established the Spanish Colonial Arts Society. Along with artist Frank Applegate, she was instrumental in saving the then private chapel, Santuario de Chimayo and granting the property to the Archdiocese of Santa Fe. She along with Ansel Adams, a well-known photographer from Carmel California, co-authored her book, *Taos Pueblo*.

Another famous writer in the cultural circle of Carmel was Sinclair Lewis, the first American writer to be given the Nobel Prize in Literature. What I later uncovered about him touched my family roots, for his wife was Grace Livingston-Hegger, staff editor of *Vogue Magazine* in New York City where her father, Frank Hegger, had an Art and Photographic Gallery. An early picture of her resembles my father. They named their son after H.G. Wells, another accomplished writer.

Grace Livingston-Hegger and son Wells.

Charles Collier enjoyed a colorful upbringing during his extended stays in New Mexico. He never forgot the elegant Casa Grande, Cottonwoods, and the Rio Grande in Los Luceros. As a young man, he was the first to show a family friend, Georgia O'Keeffe; driving the artist around in her Ford Sedan. O'Keeffe never forgot the favor and after Mary C. Wheelwright passed away bequeathing Los Luceros to Mary Chabot, who put it up for sale, she notified Charles Collier that Los Luceros was for sale. John Collier, Charles' father was a friend of Mabel Dodge Luhan from Taos. He was a Native American advocate and commissioner of Indian Affairs. He was instrumental in ending the loss of reservation lands held by the Indians.

Many others graced this land of Los Luceros such as Nathan Boone, son of Daniel Boone who camped on the grounds. Leonard Bernstein played the piano gifted by Rockefellers.

Robert Redford, director of the "Milagro Beanfield War" wanted to purchase the property for a film school.

While I was living on the property, a prequel to the original "Lonesome Dove" miniseries "Comanche Moon" was filmed here. I also felt a connection to this historical landmark. The opportunity to lead an extraordinary life was not by chance but by heavenly design—to lead a purposeful life in the course of discovering the power and energy that gave one a spirit of creativity.

Apparently, actor/director Robert Redford fell in love with Los Luceros while he was filming "Milagro Beanfield War" in the late nineteen-eighties. After which, his love of the land many perceived as sacred, gave way to a vision to create a Sundance Film Academy, similar to the one he had created in Utah. Additionally, Redford became involved with the Department of Cultural Affairs. Therefore, he was honored for his contribution to the state and its people. It is my understanding that he truly felt the specialness of the setting that over the years had served as an oasis of sorts to numerous individuals who had also experienced its specialness.

It had been said Redford hoped to give residents of New Mexico a greater voice in the film industry. Furthermore, he was especially concerned about the Native Americans who had inhabited the land initially. Although many moons have passed, the vision still lingers while others have been called to complete the task.

Thereby, there's a need to nurture the seed that has been planted, that with faith may give rise to its glory.

There is great opportunity for unique storytelling told through the lens of a unique community filled with warm hearts and divine storytelling. In bringing the academy to life and fully embracing the idea of looking forward to the future with an eye on the past, we will align ourselves with veteran creative forces such as writers, directors, and visual effects artists. Rising Sun Creative Arts Academy was created by Jay Cash who also designed the front cover of my book.

The academy serves as a creative conduit.

Preserving and sharing traditions and histories and showcasing them in a new and relevant way that would have otherwise been lost, faded, and forgotten and in turn would encourage community involvement while promoting such conservation efforts.

Entrance of Los Luceros. Photograph by Gene Peach.

Barbara's residence in Los Luceros (2005–2007). Photograph by Gene Peach.

Capia in Los Luceros. Photograph by Gene Peach.

Casa Grande in Los Luceros. Photograph by Gene Peach.

Cottonwood in Los Luceros. Photograph by Gene Peach.

Peacocks in Los Luceros. Photograph by Gene Peach.

Santuario de Chimayo. Photograph by Gene Peach.

River house in Los Luceros. Photograph by Gene Peach.

River house along the Rio Grande. Photograph by Gene Peach.

5 ~ SONORAN HERITAGE WHEAT

Matachines in Alcalde. Photograph by Gene Peach.

Sonoran heritage wheat was grown in North New Mexico. It was brought in by the Spanish expeditions and the missionaries.

Father Kino as he established Catholic missions likely introduced wheat to make communion wafers. I learned that one of the first crops they planted around Los Luceros in the late fifteen hundreds was wheat. There weaves a story of the monoculturalization of the America wheat to then diversify products to increase food production. The heritage grain of years ago were gluten free which leads to the importance of growing the wheat berry for ourselves and for our health.

How fitting that during the time of preparation of the coming of "He who is the Bread of Life," grains and bread should play a prominent role in honor of St. Barbara; feast day December 4, St. Nicholas December 6, (my daughter Kristin's birthday), St. Lucy December 13, (my son Jeffrey's birthday). Yet another synchronicity.

The St. Barbara's Branch is an ancient tradition symbolic of new life and Spring, because the barren branches bloom and turn green in the middle of winter. How fitting since Christ came as a branch from the root of Jesse.

Ron Boyd and wife Debra Clare own and operate Mer-Girl Gardens near Alcalde, New Mexico where they grow seeds such as the Glass Gem, a favorite Indian corn, rainbow hues, a bit translucent, with each kernel a different color.

Boyd has the benefit of access to the acequia for irrigation from the Los Luceros ranch. Mer-Girl is the water-bearer to them in the desert. Ron Boyd speaks with reverence of the earth, of interconnected paly of pollinators and plants, of the blessing abundant water in our often-parched desert landscape.

"The soil was getting treated like dirt."

As I sat gazing at the fireplace while taking in the peace which permeated the surrounding landscape, the flickering flames gave me a feeling of warmth and calm.

Somehow it felt as if the light of the flames held the power of hope of new beginnings whereby my eyes were drawn to a certain book on the shelf nearby which was titled *Land of Little Rain* by author Mary Hunter Austin.

Being the inquisitive person that I am, I started reading the book which held my attention down to the very last word. I wondered why the book was here. I realized later on that she along with other writers had experienced the land as well. As I continued to read whatever I could find on Mary Hunter Austin, I began to realize how several of her decisions would influence the very course of my life, ultimately paving the way for my journey as I have shared earlier. Fascinating again while reflecting on the promptings of the Holy Spirit, recounting my journey a member of Carmel's Art Community was brought to the very door of my gift shop across the way of El Santuario de Chimayo.

Being on the land as previously stated gave way to my hosting a Divine Mercy Conference with Father Pablo Straub, the officiating priest from Acapulco. Therefore, once again the land was blessed by him and his quintessential predecessor Hosteen Klah. I recently learned that the vintage seeds were planted in the land of the Morning Star, consequently holding hope for those to come.

Speaking of seed, I recently wanted to see if I could find out what was happening at Los Luceros in more recent times, as I had heard where the land was being farmed and had been planted with Heritage Seeds.

Meanwhile, my search led to the following discovery as I read where the Sonoran Heritage Wheat that had been planted in Northern New Mexico had been brought by Spaniards and missionaries, who likely used the wheat to make communion wafers. As I continued to read the cover story, that I had found in the Santa Fe Reporter, the name Ron Boyd who had commented throughout the article, somehow felt eerily familiar. There, woven like the baskets of the nearby Native Americans amid a story of multiculturalization to diversify products in a bid to increase food production, was yet another unexpected discovery.

Whereby it suddenly dawned upon me that some time back, I had actually spoken to Ron Boyd when I called to see if I might purchase a kaleidoscope like the ones I had carried in my gift shop years earlier.

Furthermore, I had been to his home as his lovely wife was the individual who created the kaleidoscopes I sold.

As memory once again gave way to form, I recalled my having commented on a photograph of a distinguished gentleman.

After which Debra Claire (the lady of the house hold) advised me, the gentleman was her great-great-grandfather Louis B Mayer, who co-founded MGM Studios.

What I found rather ironic was when I shared the incident with Glenda Finn, she then told me another story. It seems

Glenda's mentor writer/screenwriter Ivan Goff was friends with Louis B Mayer and his son-in-law David Selznick. The relationship between Selznick and Goff was enduring for Selznick came to Ivan's rescue when some haughty more accomplished screenwriter had attempted to intimidate the young man that Selznick had invited to join them for dinner. Adding to the intrigue was the fact I was wanting to purchase the kaleidoscope as a gift for Glenda who was my connection to Nouveaux Reign Entertainment.

Years later, as my father was getting up in years, he would love to come to visit my husband and we loved his visits. He attended mass with us, after forty years, and was pleased that his daughter sang in the Spanish choir with her Hispanic husband. He and my husband were the best of friends and did little favors for each other.

I remember when he told us about the time he stopped at a popular fast-food place on the way to our house where he noticed a sign that read free WiFi, so when he picked up his order, he asked the person at the cash register if he could throw in a few of those free WiFis. He was a character and always had a story to share.

A few years ago, his visit was different, he seemed sad and told us that this would be his last visit. I told him if he came back then we would have a birthday party for him the next year. The morning he was leaving, as he started to the front door, I said, "wait, where is my hug." I felt it was my last and that I would never see him again. He had told us that he was having heart problems, for he would always claim that he was going to live to be a hundred. A month later, the call came. He had a major heart attack and passed on.

The choir director and his wife had become very good friends of ours and asked us to bring a picture of my father to their house for the novena of poor souls, which lasted for nine days. I agreed, and on the fifth day of the novena, I awoke from a very lucid dream about my father.

My father was holding me in his arms for what seemed like hours. I felt it strange that he was wearing one man's shoe and one woman's high healed shoe. He asked me if I would bring him his other man's shoe, and I did. It was not like a dream for the place was gray and seemed real. I felt he was reaching out to me for some reason and shared this with my husband. Heaven knows what this meant but I have peace with whatever it was. His mission had ended on this earth.

Meanwhile, memories of my travels to other countries, like the golden nuggets began to reappear, and as always, put me in a state of spiritual wonder. Whereby I recalled a mountainous road with hairpin turns, and our tour bus arriving at a hamlet in Spain. We had been invited to join another group of about fifty people to listen to an Irish mystic lighthouse keeper give a talk on the Blessed Virgin Mary.

As he came near the end of his speech, he described the precious jewels in "Our Ladies" crown as amber. He said it was a much more brilliant hue of orange and deep yellow, unlike the amber we know of here. After which he held up an amber-colored rosary and gave it to me. The gift of the rosary brought back the recollection of the mystery of my missing rosary, the special rosary from Medjugorje with a chain that had turned from silver to gold. Perhaps this was the Blessed Mother's way of asking me to say more rosaries.

Following his talk, many people surrounded him. Therefore, we had started to leave when he suddenly reached out and put his hand on my shoulder saying, "Wait, I want to talk to you." After the crowd dispersed, he asked me if I knew why I was given the rosary? I told him that I had concluded that it was the replacement of a rosary I had lost or perhaps I was being lax in praying the rosary and Our Lady wanted me to pray the rosary more often. He left it at that, but I have always wondered why he had given me the rosary.

A few years later, I decided to search for his name in Ireland and to my surprise, I found him and his contact information. I rang him and explained to him that I was the lady he gave the amber-colored rosary to in Spain a few years earlier. He replied that he did remember giving me the special rosary and that the Holy Spirit had prompted him to give it to me. I was not only surprised but very happy to have been so honored by an apparent gift from God. I thanked him and wished him well.

Not long after that, I wrote a prayer for lost children. I combined it with a beautiful picture of St. Anthony holding Jesus with a single pink rose. St. Therese's signal to me was always the single pink rose but now St Anthony, I thought St. Anthony was always shown with the lily. Maybe St. Anthony and St. Therese are working together for the children.

Prayer to St. Anthony for Our Children

Loveable St. Anthony, we come to you, with complete childlike confidence, as a favor before God, who heeds your pleas for those in need.

Dear St. Anthony, loving protector, defender of the innocent, in trust we place in your arms our children, who often are victims of abuse, neglect, and violence.

Prayer for their protection. Pray that those innocent victims, who suffer for the sins of others, be returned for our safe-keeping.

Pray for our peace of mind, to carry on this special mission, and comfort us in our time of loss.

Pray for all of us who have lost faith, hope, and friendship with God, so that we may have new faith, new hope, and new love.

Dear St. Anthony, procure for us steadfastness, and determination to make this nation a safer haven for our children.

In your kindness and compassion, consider these and all the prayers of your innocent children, and carry them up to heaven above, for the blessings on our troubled, unloved, and unwanted.

Quiet the fears of our precious children and return peace and security in their hearts.

Saint Anthony with a single pink rose.

My friends, who traveled many times to Medjugorje, started a Peace Cenacle in their home and invited close to seventy people to their home for a guest speaker who gave talks on Guardian Angels. My friends had brought me a beautiful multicolored rosary from Medjugorje the year before and since the chain had recently turned gold, I was excited to show my friends the rosary and maybe tell the speaker, author of the book, *The Light of Lovely* by Patricia Devlin, although blind, she could see light, even though she had no eyes. For spiritually, she could see more than anyone there.

As I was handing her the rosary, I noticed that the corpus on the cross had moved down to the foot of the cross and His head was below the metal marking where his head had rested against. I told the blind lady that the body moved down the cross while I handed her my rosary and she said, no the body of Jesus on the crucifix was moving while I was walking up to her, which was probably at least ten feet away from her.

Many there witnessed the changed rosary.

The same lady that gave me the rosary that turned gold had invited me to her land in Winterset, Iowa, the birthplace of actor John Wayne. She and her husband had a magnificent life-size statue of the Blessed Mother, set in a woodsy area amongst the beautiful oak trees and butterflies that danced with joy, fluttering about surrounding a white alabaster statue of the Blessed Mother. The serenity of it all made you feel you just wanted to stay there forever.

As we knelt in prayer, our eyes fixated on her image, when suddenly Her pure white hands that were folded in prayer, turned pink. What an amazing grace we received that beautiful summer day. Meanwhile, my friend who taught nursing at the nearby college, prior to her retirement, asked me to ride along with her to a property she owned in Missouri, for she needed to close it for the winter.

We had a great time driving along the countryside when we realized that a lovely monarch butterfly got caught in the windshield wiper, we stopped and removed it, after which we gave it a proper burial. As we were driving along, we noticed that another beautiful monarch butterfly was flying around inside the car. We thought perhaps it got on board at the filling station since the windows were closed the whole time. It eventually lighted on my hair. I had assumed the enchanting butterfly would eventually leave but on the contrary, it remained with me for the duration of my journey.

Due to the unusual occurrence, I did a little research and discovered that the sudden appearance of butterflies suggests the presence of one's Guardian Angel. They are messengers of the spiritual and angelic world. A blessed journey we had with the Monarch, a sign from our guardian Angels, protecting us on our travels. They are graceful but silent. It brought to my mind El Santuario de Chimayo, the sacred historic site, which is nestled near the Sangre de Cristo Mountains in the heart of El Potrero in New Mexico.

Before the Spanish came, this spiritual place was considered a sacred place by the Pueblo and Tewa Indians since the twelfth century, when they inhabited these lands. The Tewa named Chimayo "Tsi Mayoh" after one of the four sacred hills above the valley which lay directly behind the Santuario (Sanctuary). Chimayo lies in the valley made fertile by the Rio Santa Cruz (Holy Cross River). The area is noted for its orchards, chili peppers, pinon, and wonderful weavings.

Chimayo was once volcanic and left behind hot springs that eventually vanished and left behind a pool of mud. The Tewa recognized its healing properties and blessed earth. Later when the Spanish settlers arrived in El Postrero, a cross was found buried on the property and later permission was given to build a chapel on the site in honor of the miraculous image of the dark-skinned Christ on the crucifix of Esquipulas. The Santuario was privately owned until 1929 when the Spanish Colonial Art Society in Santa Fe kept it from demolition.

Writer, Mary Hunter Austin, and several others purchased the Santuario from the family and donated it to the Archdiocese of Santa Fe. After retiring from years of confinement, I felt free at last to travel to the southwest, which had always intrigued me.

As I was passing through New Mexico, taking the back roads to Taos, I came across a sign on the road that read El Santuario de Chimayo. My curiosity got the best of me; so, I decided to stop and pay a little visit to the famous pilgrimage church in the heart of Chimayo. As I recall, I had immediate chills pass over me as I entered the quaint church built in 1816, where a four-hundred-year-old carving of Christ towered over me. As I walked around the grounds, I saw a fence built with several little wooden crosses affixed to it.

I went on to visit the little chapel of the Santo Nino Atocha. In the infant room were rows of baby shoes dedicated to the child Jesus of Atocha. Across from the church was a lovely small cottage trimmed in turquoise; begging for me to peer into the window; whereby I learned that the building was vacant; and then realized that a few steps in the back of the building, there was a home and so I rang the doorbell. A pleasant elderly lady came to the door.

I inquired about the vacant building and wondered who owned it. She replied happily that it was hers; but since her husband's passing, it was left vacant for years; but asked if I would be interested in making it a gift shop? So, without even thinking about it, I said yes. Mind you, I was on vacation, and I certainly knew nothing about owning a gift shop nor did I know the culture there.

Sadie asked me to come to see her the next day so we could have coffee and discuss some more about the gift shop.

The next morning while we were enjoying the coffee in each other's company, she said "I guess you are wondering why I asked you to make my property a gift shop? Well, every year in the spring, all the neighbors plant their signs on my property, to attract the pilgrims to their retail establishments. So, I finally told them no more signs because I was going to have a gift shop. Well, I lied, I really did not have any intentions of opening a gift shop, so the day you appeared at my home was the day I had planned to go to confession, but you agreed to make it a gift shop and now I do not need to go to confession because I did not lie; rather it was a foretelling of what God had intended." Her only request was that I would name the shop "El Potrero" for which I had a sign made and set outside the door.

Needless to say, a letter from an attorney came to me; expressing that his client would sue us since his shop across the street was named Potrero Trading Post. I did not want to cause any problems so I just called it a "Gift Shop." I also put on my sign that I had an in-house artist make, one that I did not have at the time; but a few weeks before I opened the gift shop, a local artist, Fernando Bimonte, entered my shop for a place to display his work and do custom work for the pilgrims. The altar that he painted is now in our chapel.

6 ~ GOD'S HIDDEN HAND

Meanwhile, word of miracles and the Holy Ground, as well as, references to God's power and goodness spread quickly. Therefore, people soon traveled, often great distances, in search of a miracle. My thoughts took me to the mystery of the crucifix and how this played a major role in the conversion of many near the place of the Sangre de Cristo Mountains (the blood of Christ) and the water of the Santa Cruz River.

The Indians from these holy grounds contributed to the sanctification of the world through the Great White Spirit in the sky (The Holy Spirit). The illumination of the cross, showing God's Hidden Hand was this church's special mission. And St. Therese's hand was bringing me here to New Mexico for my part, in my mission to continue down the path God created for me.

I reflect on my first communion day when, like St. Therese, I gave myself to Jesus and wanted so much to be with Him in Heaven. Solitary moments like these help reflect on being highly honored by the nuns for choosing me to be the Blessed Mother in our Christmas play.

I also recall how disappointed I felt when I had not been chosen to crown the Blessed Mother for May Day. I loved the month of May because we had our May altar adorned with little vases of roses and lilacs, and sometimes Easter would arrive in the same month. I loved the Stations of the Cross, Holy Thursday washing of the feet, Blessing of the Paschal Candle, Blessing of the Palms, and Good Friday—the kissing of the Crucifix, and of course beautiful Easter morning when Jesus rose from the cross, to be our Redeemer. A more exciting and fulfilling life was never lasting in the life of the world.

Christ dwells in our hearts by the Holy Spirit when we say yes to him, carrying us when we follow him, and strengthening us with his many Graces. I am a firm believer that first impressions are lasting impressions.

The first movie on the big screen for me to see was "The Ten Commandments," which impressed upon my mind the role Christianity played on the world stage. Each child is a unique little flower; our children are affected by what they see on the movie screen. As children, we were limited to two channels where our minds are being formed at an early age. Throughout my life, I have had great concern and compassion for our innocent children, therefore I wrote a prayer to St. Anthony, which is a part of my story.

St. Therese herself inspired me to write this book and share with you her special charisms of wisdom. "To live in love is to sail forever, spreading seeds of joy and peace in hearts." "Love gives people a reason for living and a sense of hope."

Sometimes we need to get out of our comfort zone and go out on a limb to make a difference in someone's life. Just as the acorn contains the mighty oak tree, the self has everything it needs to fulfill its destiny. When the inner conditions are right, it naturally emerges. The tallest oak in the forest was once a tiny nut that held its ground, so like the oak tree, we need to hold our ground, for tough love can be the tiny seed that fills the earth with fields of flowers.

We don't need to see to believe but we need to believe to see... My friend Glenda Finn wrote a special note, "Whereby the mammoth oak will undoubtedly have seen many a season, note that the concentric rings in its core will forever reveal the conditions it has experienced." Go with the branch, with the life, in where the dead branches fall away. The sky is the limit when you view your life from above. See God's Hidden Hand in everything and you will never be disappointed.

As fate would have it, my supposed vacation to the southwest and ultimately northern New Mexico would subsequently lead me to the very essence of my life mission; which is to bring every culture into unity and love. Meanwhile, the gift shop became a means through which I not only met individuals from the far corners of the earth but furthered my mission.

For the most part, those who visited the Gift Shop and Chimayo were believers that were intent on worshipping Christ and the Saints, although, there were others who were merely curious as to why thousands would travel from far and wide to visit a site many perceived as Holy.

Once inside the mission, few could deny the amazing power held in faith for crutches, baby shoes, and other items that were left behind, while visitors frequently left, free of their earlier maladies. Having observed their expressions and subsequent job, I was consistently reminded of the power of one's testimony that had to further their faith.

Therefore, I began thinking I might one day recount my journey in book form so that it could inspire hope in others, as well as, pay tribute to St. Therese, my patroness who time and time again has made her presence known.

It brought to mind the mystery held in the acorns that I gathered in my youth which ultimately gave rise to the mighty oak. Thus, giving way to letting go and letting God direct my life; for he knew me better than I knew myself. My heart gave way to letting go and letting God direct my life.

Once I gave up my control of life, everything fell into place; for God opened all the doors I needed to fulfill my purpose in life. The joy and the overwhelming peace that I feel from the Holy Spirit's direction, not mine, is a grace and blessing available to anyone who asks.

I would have probably missed the opportunity to open this gift shop had it not been for St. Therese, patroness of missions, and her novena promise to let fall from heaven a shower of roses; her hidden hand from heaven doing good upon the earth. I may never even had recognized this special gift from God. He allows love to transform me to do everything in love and confidence.

In the heart of El Potrero, across the street from my little gift shop, is El Santuario de Chimayo. Around the early 1800s, a friar was hearing confessions when he saw a light bursting from the hillside. Digging, he found a crucifix of Esquipulas Guatemala. A local priest brought the crucifix to Santa Cruz Church, but it disappeared three times and was traced back to the hole it had been buried in; so, a small chapel was built on this site which later became the place from where the pilgrims would scoop up the adobe-colored dirt and take it with them.

Eventually, a larger mission church was built known as the "Lourdes of America." The Holy Dirt had to be brought in from the nearby Sangre de Cristo Mountains, from the nearby hillside. In the Holy Dirt Room hangs the beautifully framed picture of St. Therese, the Little Flower, which graces the wall above the entrance.

In 1929, a member of the Spanish Colonial Arts Society, Mary Hunter Austin, was instrumental in keeping the mission church from being demolished and donated it to the Archdiocese of Santa Fe. The *Washington Post* reported that the National Park Service had called the site one of the most important Catholic Pilgrimage Centers in the United States. Being a National Historic Landmark, the TV Show "Miracle Detectives" analyzed the soil and found high levels of calcium carbonate; but could not explain the extraordinary healing properties of the Holy Dirt of Chimayo.

Priests claimed the healing was one of faith and not the dirt. Another priest, Father Jim, claimed that people, upon having discovered that there was something special here, opened up in their hearts. The history of the "El Pocito" goes back two hundred years. The crutches hanging on the wall, were discarded by those that claimed to heal here, the pictures of servicemen, and others, as well as the sick, adorn the wall; the beautiful statue of the Santo Nino de Atocha where a kneeler sits, is for those who want to pray.

Near the mission church is the Children's Chapel of the Santo Nino de Atocha. The story of the pilgrim Jesus originates in Atocha, Spain, where reports of Atocha children returning from prison were that an unknown boy dressed as a pilgrim, who was carrying a gourd of water, and loaves of bread, was feeding the prisoners. The people soon became convinced that this was the child Jesus, who was sent by his mother. When the people went to the chapel to give thanks, it was noted that the shoes of the infant Jesus were worn and dirty. As often as they were replaced with new shoes, they too became dirty and worn. This was proof to the people of the nightly excursions of the infant in helping those in need. He became known as the "Santo Nino de Atocha."

The family of the Abteya, due to miraculous healing, promised a shrine to the Santo Nino. It was granted, and soon the children's chapel was constructed on these holy grounds and is still a highlight of this pilgrimage site. I remember Fr. Jim telling a group of us that before Fr. Jorge Bergoglio became Pope, he and his sister visited the Santuario in Chimayo. I had wondered why he had flown all that way to visit this humble mission church El Santuario de Chimayo, the sacred historic site, nestled near the Sangre de Cristo mountains in the heart of El Potrero in New Mexico.

The well-preserved small adobe mission church brings thousands of pilgrims, the valley's faithful, and the occasional sightseer. The approach to the church is through the double doorway set into a thick adobe wall. Its interior is a colorful mixture of Spanish and Indian culture, Hispanic religious folk art, Santos, and religious frescoes. Behind the altar stands the six foot Crucifix of Our Lord of Esquipulas. Then to your left are two separate rooms. The walls of one room adorn pictures of service people, and expressions of thanks for healings of the mind, body, and spirit.

Crutches, crosses, and rosaries of all colors rest near statues and benches. In the other very small room, "El Pocito," is the little well of the blessed dirt that was brought in from the foothills of the mountains.

When I entered the little room to fill my little container with Holy Dirt, I thought it marvelous that a framed picture of my favorite, Saint Therese, was hanging there and that another large picture was standing on the ground, a matter of two feet from the well of dirt. How odd since these were the only pictures of saints in that little room.

Nearby the church is a children's chapel of Santo Nino Atocha. Many baby shoes line the inner room, for the story goes that the pilgrim child would visit the prisoners and give them water and bread, and would wear out his shoes so the tradition of taking to him the shoes was in thanksgiving to the Santo Nino Atocha.

A more recent sculpture, the three culture monument, depicts the gathering of the Native Americans, the Anglo Cowboys, and the Hispanic Vaquero, under the benevolent figure of the Blessed Virgin Mary. Many other additions have been made in the past few years, including remodeling of the Santo Nino Chapel, and added gift shops, among other improvements. The blending of traditions and cultures shows the open hearts of the pilgrims.

Investigative files reports "El Santuario de Chimayo, Lourdes of North America."

After I had secured the rental agreement with the owner for a gift shop, it became evident that I had my work cut out for me. For starters, I would have to post my intent to open a business for several months before I could even attempt to ready the place for the grand opening. The opening would be during the Holy Week which was when thousands of pilgrims walked from near and far, on pilgrimage. In the mean time I had to figure out what would sell in my gift shop since the culture here is quite different than my own. Furthermore, I realized I had no place to live plus I was literally a stranger here. After I attended Mass in nearby Albuquerque, a nice couple befriended me and asked me to join them for lunch at a local restaurant. In the course of the conversation the fact that I was looking for a place to rent came up and they suggested I talk to a local priest that they knew well.

After which they assured me that he would help me.

The next morning, I appeared at the rectory and asked the secretary to see the priest and she ushered me into his office. What a gracious compassionate priest he was. Realizing my plight, he called one of his parishioners about a rental but it was no longer available. So, the father asked me if I had ever seen a Capia and of course I said I didn't know what this was. He smiled as he suggested he would show me. As we started to drive down the road things eventually became rural. We were subsequently met by massive cottonwoods, wildflowers and a sign that read "Historic Los Luceros," and one of the most magnificent 19th century ranches ever.

A short while after we had entered the gate, Fr. Brennan pointed out the Capia, the charming small chapel surrounded by crimson wildflowers. As I recall I felt a sense of awe as I saw the scattering of primarily adobe structures that also graced the property, some of which had lilacs, and pink rose bushes adorning their landscape. Furthermore, two burros greeted us as we passed them which added to our feeling of being welcomed by a dream to a setting one might think was reminiscent of the Garden of Eden.

The presence of hundreds of apple trees on the 137 acres of formal gardens laden with fruit, a variety of garden vegetables and herbs suggested everything one might ever need was here. It was obviously planned to be that way. Brilliant colored peacocks of blue and green iridescent plumage opened themselves to us in all their glory for our pleasure. A sudden appearance of fluffy white cottontail rabbits came out of hiding to see what all the commotion was about.

Los Luceros was a place of peace and tranquility, set on the banks of the Rio Grande River. The hidden hacienda was on the National Register of Historic Places.

Amongst other things, it featured a two- story river house with a wraparound deck, plus the beautiful Casa Ground House which was at one time part of the Court House. The history of the ranch goes back as far as the 1920s when Mary Cabot Wheelwright, art heiress from New England roots purchased it for a ranch where soon many famous people like the artist Georgia O'Keeffe, known for her paintings of enlarged flowers and New Mexico landscapes became a special guest here.

Ansel Adams, famous photographer, had visited the Casa Grande House on the property. She belonged to the New Mexico Historical Society and the Wheelwright Museum is named after her.

Historic Los Luceros includes five adobe structures, including the Casa Grande which served as the County Courthouse in the middle 1800s. It also includes a Pueblo Indian ruin, tucked on the Rio Grande banks near the hamlet of Alcalde. Placitas of a café, visitor center, book store and gift shop, as well as a guest house at times were used for photography retreats and conferences.

The bosque behind the adobes reminded of me the woods behind my childhood home, which immediately brought back fond memories. Therefore, I said, this is where I want to be; after which I added I would give my right arm to live there. Father Brennan said he would see what he could do. He noted there were several adobe houses that were vacant. He said he would call his friend the custodian Martin Guillon.

He called him immediately and Martin told him, "Yes, for you father I will do it." I right away thought it interesting that this custodian's name was Martin Guillon, for I knew that St. Therese's last name was Martin and her mother's last name was Guerin, pronounced the same. It of course reminded me that my patron saint of missions had somehow intervened.

To top it all off, Fr. Brennan told me there would be a guard at night protecting me (my very own Guardian Angel).

In a matter of one year, a movie was being filmed here. Another episode of "Lonesome Dove" with the movie "Comanche Moon" with Karl Urban, Steve Zahn, and Val Kilmer. The bosque behind the river house was a wooded area perfect for the branding scene; for they had to haul in the cattle and horses for this special scene. I was fascinated about all the workings of making a movie. I was only a matter of a few feet away from the directors and actors and got to observe as long as I maintained my distance from the scene. One of the cows took off and later had to be found; it evoked an earlier childhood memory when the cows got out of the fence in our woods.

A year later I decided that this beautiful land would be a great place to host a Divine Mercy Conference with my friend Father Pablo Straub, who you may remember from EWTN as always carrying the large cross. He came with his sixteen1nuns who stayed in the Rio Grande House. Father Pablo Straub stayed at the rectory and gave talks at the church the night before the conference. My friend Melissa, who played the guitar and sang at the mass at the church was accompanied by her cousin Richard Romero, and they played very beautifully and were a great addition to the celebration.

The Knights of Columbus stood at guard during the exposition of the Holy Sacrament in the Capia. My precious time in this spiritual environment, allowing me daily access to the beautiful chapel to pray was out of this world. Many came and took part in the mass and the luncheon afterwards.

The placita area could accommodate large crowds and the people enjoyed strolling around the grounds taking in the peace of this very spiritual place.

To my surprise Richard, came up to me during the luncheon and asked me if he could take me out to lunch. Well not now, this was my conference and I would not be open to leaving. He quietly walked away. I remember thinking that this man is like a man I have never come in contact with; so gentle but yet so firm. Someone told me later that day that Richard had given two white classical guitars to the nuns. Not only was he kind but generous as well! After the conference things quieted down, and I was again enveloped in the serenity of the beauty that surrounded me that felt removed from the rest of the world, I suddenly felt myself whereby I thought perhaps finding true love was not just a dream.

Barbara Hegger-Romero with some cast members from the movie, "Comanche Moon," filmed in historic Los Luceros.

7 ~ FINDING HOPE AND PEACE

Rev: 22:2—"Leaves of the Tree were for healing of the nations."
Drawing by my husband, Richard Romero, of an oak tree and acorn.

Countless visitors came through the door of my gift shop, for it was indeed welcoming listening to their stories of finding hope and peace at the pilgrimage site, meanwhile, others shared they were praying for loved ones or seeking guidance in their lives. The customers included a young mother looking for an infant coral bracelet for protection, parents looking for items for their children's baptism, confirmation, first communion, marriage, or a unique handmade rosary or cross. Many children came in for medals and other items; I always gave them some saint's holy card or a little container for the holy dirt. I was in my element sharing the history behind the sacred site, the story of the pilgrim boy Jesus of Atocha, and how he would help the needy and feed the prisoners.

Sharing such stories made it all the more interesting, therefore I profited greatly as I inspired others. I even had made up a story scroll for every customer that purchased the large wooden and tin crosses, small altars, and tin Christmas ornaments, all created by a local artist using the tin from the old roof of the church. Another artist painted tiles of saints, while another made unique jewelry. People came from all over the world while worshiping Jesus.

The neighboring shop was a gift shop and restaurant that featured outdoor dining. The chef was also my artist. We had music for a special event; I invited the vocalist from church and her cousin Richard Romero, an accomplished musician to sing and play their guitars on the patio of my gift shop, entertaining the visitors while they strolled along the grounds of the pilgrimage site.

Their performance was quite a hit. I had seen Richard before, on Divine Mercy Sunday, with his cousin leading the procession outside of the church. I figured he had to be happily married; for he looked serene and at the same time charming, and charismatic. After the musical event, he came in and asked me if I would like to go out with him. Although I was too scared to say yes. Then I wondered if he was married, or had a girlfriend.

A month later I had the Divine Mercy Conference at the Historic Los Luceros where I resided; and of course, my friend and her cousin Richard led the choir for the mass.

After mass lunch was served, and I was quite busy when all of a sudden Richard asked me if I would like to go somewhere for lunch? To which I replied; Thank you, but I cannot leave this conference. Later on, my friend told me that Richard's mother had just passed away. I told her, of course, I wanted to be there to give him my condolences, so she asked me to sit with her where she would be singing for the mass.

After mass, I came up to him, and expressed my condolences, for which he quickly kissed me on the cheek. A week later, following mass, I went to the adoration chapel to pray, I had grasped the handle of the entrance door, only to feel the warm hand of Richard sweetly caressing and covering mine. He had caught me by surprise. I turned to him and suddenly the Pardon Crucifix I was wearing around my neck came off the chain and fell to the ground. To my amazement, he quickly gathered it up and put it in his pocket... Later that June we had a walk against drugs event, and all who participated were invited to a barbeque at the church social hall. I asked Richard if he would like to accompany me and he said yes. By this time, I felt he must still be interested in me; but I had sworn off men, so I was in no way wanting a relationship that could cause me heartache. I had asked him when his birthday was and he said June 21st, perfect.

Then I asked him, "How would you and your daughter and your two grandchildren like to have dinner at my house in Los Luceros. I like to cook and this way we can get to know each other better."

The dinner was fabulous, we sat across the table from each other looking into each other's eyes with a magnetism, unlike anything I have experienced, feeling a spiritual mysticism beyond this earthly plane. We instantly knew we would always be together no matter where our lives would take us, it was a bond sealed in heaven. We had a great time, his daughter was very gracious, and his granddaughters were very polite. Soon we were an item, we had fun being together, going to the mountains, taking part in his music gigs, meeting his friends, discovering instances of synchronicity, like me coming from Chicago to New Mexico, and his father nicknamed Chicago because he was from Chicago; Richard taking me to meet his best friend from St. Catherine's Indian School, Moonlighter, who I knew as Ivan Garcia, my rosary maker; telling me about his aunt Sr. Mary Louise, same as the nun's name that lived near me in Iowa, whereby the priest that had lived next to me Fr. Ricardo was also Richard's professional name. At one time I shared with him my devotion to St. Therese the Little Flower, and how I had prayed at the reliquary of St. Therese which toured the Carmelite Monasteries around the United States. Pope John Paul II had proclaimed her one of the Doctors of the Church a few years before. Her reliquary would be arriving at the Carmelite Monastery in Sioux City, Iowa. I prayed to my St. Therese Novena and prayed at the Reliquary that was placed in the chapel honoring her.

Later, sharing this with Richard, his eyes sparkled when he exclaimed "That's nothing, I helped carry that same St Therese reliquary in the Carmelite Monastery in Santa Fe where my aunt is a nun there." In fact, he added, he was considering becoming a Carmelite Brother, to which I responded, "I also was contemplating becoming a Lay Carmelite." Therefore, we feel Saint Therese brought us together and gave us a special mission together. Years later we received the sacrament of matrimony, and with God's grace, we hope to bring love and happiness to our families and all those that God has put before us, with good intentions and heartfelt thanks to all who have accepted us.

Sometimes God gives you things you didn't even ask for because he knows us better than we know ourselves. As St. Therese says, "Holiness consists simply in doing God's will, and being just what God wants us to be."

"God does not need years to accomplish His work of love in a soul; one ray from His heart can, in an instant, make His flower bloom for eternity."

I vividly remember the day Richard showed me the Pardon Crucifix that he had kept, making me feel like I was very special to him. Sometimes when I would look into his eyes I would have to look away; for his eyes were the window to his soul. Once I glimpsed into his heart, I felt we shared a love I knew would last forevermore. My father visited me often and became very close to Richard, who eventually asked permission from my father for my hand in marriage. Being that we came from different cultures I had to communicate to my father that this was his culture. At first, he did not understand, this gesture was new to him but with my help, he realized he needed to respond in truth, kindness, and respect.

Our wedding day, Valentine's Day 2013.

8 ~ OF BODY AND BLOOD

I find it fascinating how the Holy Spirit over time would reveal our shared interest as well as the unending interest of our patron saint, St. Therese in the Holy Face and the Shroud of Turin. In the course of recounting my journey, I was seeking information on Father Ricardo about seeking his permission to mention him in my book that pays tribute to St. Therese and the intercession of saints. To my amazement, I stumbled upon his address from a website of a retreat house that had hosted Father for lectures on the Shroud of Turin that he had studied for over thirty years.

In contemplating the mass, I was made aware of the reason why the sanctuary was set up the way it was. The altar linens of the liturgy on the altar stone, which in earlier times was offered on the tomb of a saint, the cloth called Sindon (shroud) has the theological connection with the real presence of Jesus in the Eucharist which is the celebration connection with the real presence of Jesus in the Eucharist, the center of the celebration of the mass. This leads us to the beginning of the church, the last supper, the body and blood of Christ, and the Eucharist itself. The Shroud, the burial cloth of Jesus called (Sindon) would therefore be understood as the relic's direct expression of personified real presence on the altar which biblically confirms the evidence of Jesus Christ's resurrection in the mystery of the transformation of the body and blood called transubstantiation. The corporal (Sudarium), meaning face cloth must be folded in a certain way via the analogy of the sudarium found by Peter and John in the empty tomb, not lying with the linen cloth but rolled up or folded in a separate place.

St. Therese's little way is simplicity itself, detached from worldly things and therefore leading one to joy, meekness, and humility of the heart...

Humility is being content to be who, where, and what God asks of us today, an empty vessel to be filled by Him. He loves us forever and wants us to turn our eyes toward

His face. "Truly I tell you, anyone, who will not receive the kingdom of God as a little child will never enter it" (Mark 10:15). A humble heart rests confidently in His mercy and love, no longer in fear of being little or unnoticed, realizing each day is a gift towards holiness for ordinary people.

As Saint Therese says, "We ought to be like roses in the midst of thorns, which however they are pricked or pierced, never to lose their sweet gentle fragrance. The love of God is the brilliant color of the flowers, the bright hues of the rainbow, the precious stones of the crown, the sparkle of the diamond, the most perfect and pure."

The choices we make, whether it be self- will or uniting our will with God's divine will actually determine the outcome of our life's journey.

Saint Therese's Devotion to the Holy Face

St. Therese together with her whole family were registered as members of the Archconfraternity of Reparation of the Holy Face at Tours, France. Sister Mary of St. Peter through whom our Lord gave us this devotion, that she wore a relic of her hair, and carried her picture in her New Testament which she kept close to her heart. While lying sick in the infirmary, with the picture of the Holy Face hung upon the curtains of her bed, "Who has believed our message and to whom has the arm of the Lord been revealed?" (Isaiah 53:1)

The Shroud and the Sudarium were found and discovered first by the apostles Peter and John; we can be sure are the two clothes present in the liturgy. They were stored for many years in the East and were always hidden. The depiction of the face of Jesus on these clothes would therefore be understood as the direct expression and personified "Real Presence of Jesus" on the altar and directly related to the Eucharist as the center of the Holy Mass. Hence, biblically confirmed evidence of Christ's resurrection. The altar cloth was to be of pure linen as are the burial cloths showing the stigmata and face of Jesus on the sudarium. The corporal is the starched cloth that signifies the cloth rolled up in a separate place, not lying with the linen cloths.

The blessed face was the mirror wherein she beheld the heart and soul of her well-beloved. Just as the picture of a loved one serves to bring the whole person before us, so in the Holy Face of Christ, Therese beheld the humanity of Jesus Christ. We can say that this devotion was the burning inspiration of the Saint's life. St. Therese and her family were advocates of the Archconfraternity of the Holy Face, established by Pope Leo XIII in the year 1885.

Before the Revelation of the first photograph, St. Therese writes, "The just will recognize Him not only by the Cross but by the symbol of salvation that will precede His coming, more exactly, by His face, which will shine on the last day."

Today, the saint is another "Doctor of the Church."

Eucharist, which is the center of the mass, leads us to the beginning of the church, the Eucharist, and the body and blood of Christ. The shroud and the sudarium of Jesus would therefore be understood as the relic's direct expression personified by the real presence on the altar which biblically confirms the evidence of Jesus Christ's resurrection in the mystery of the transformation to body and blood called transubstantiation.

The corporal must be folded in a certain way by the way of analogy with the sudarium which was found by Peter and John in the empty tomb, not lying with the linen cloth but rolled up or folded in a separate place.

A chasuble painted by St. Therese and made from a dress that belonged to her mother, a deep green shade with two roses at the bottom, to represent her parents, the five lilies surrounding the Holy Face of Jesus of the Shroud are the five girls with the lily of Therese on the left. The four buds symbolize her little siblings that died at a young age.

In this life, it is necessary to undergo suffering to view our Lord's face through a veil in order to be prepared to see Him face to face in heaven. When Therese was quite young, her sister Celine and she were on a pilgrimage to Rome and a few days earlier were accompanied by their father to the Basilica of Our Lady of Victories Chapel in Paris, France; built by King Louis the thirteenth in thanksgiving to the Blessed Virgin Mary.

Young Therese Martin prayed before the statue of Our Lady of Victory for help in realizing her vocation. This was the same Basilica where her father had a novena prayed for her recovery of a grave illness when she was ten and his prayers were answered. In thanksgiving, Therese gave her gold bracelet to be melted down for a monstrance that was being made. Yes, the little way of Therese cannot be understood apart from Therese's devotion to the Holy Face. Her sister, Celine, named Sister Genevieve of the Holy Face, was taken to the summit of love and the sun, which gives strength to them as it is the divine brilliance of heaven…

"Just as the sun shines on all the trees and flowers as if each were the only one on earth, so does God care for all souls in a special manner."

Letter from St. Therese to Leonie, November 5th, 1893.

Consider the oaks of our countryside, how crooked they are; they thrust their branches to the right and left, and nothing checks them so they never reach a great height. On the other hand, consider the oaks of the forest, which are hemmed in on all those shapeless branches that rob it of the sap needed to lift it aloft. It sees only heaven, so all its strength is turned in that direction, and soon it attains a prodigious height. In religious life, the soul is like the young oak that is hemmed in on all sides by its rule. All its movements are hampered, interfered with by other trees... But it has light when it looks towards heaven, there alone it can rest its gaze, never upon anything below, it need not be afraid of rising too high...

"I am the oak tree in the acorn before it is planted, I am the child."

"Tears are the safety valve of the heart when too much pressure is laid upon it."

A Call to a Deeper Love

How many souls might attain great sanctity if only they were directed right from the start as Jesus allows a clever gardener to cultivate rare and delicate plants; giving them the tools to accomplish it. We are all flowers planted on the earth whereby God will gather us in His own good time.

A call to a deeper love, a divine love, hidden and mysterious, in which case the spirit of truth revealed to the little ones is hidden from the wise. A deeper love requires trust and surrender. A deeper prayer requires more than folding one's hands and reciting something but an outpouring from one's heart.

St. Therese experienced a deeper love through the image of the holy face of Jesus which is like a stamp applied to the soul, through prayer, and has the power of imprinting the image of God.

On the day of her clothing, she took on the name St. Therese of the Infant Jesus and the Holy Face, for she experienced great joy when gazing at the Holy Face of Jesus.

Her sister Celine wrote, "Devotion to the Holy Face was, for Therese, the crown and complement of her love for the Sacred. Through the intercession of Therese, the lives of many people have been permanently changed. Her love for us is immeasurable, and her intervention often leaves us with gratitude and appreciation. The following experiences of intercession are examples of how St. Therese continues to shower her roses upon us.

These words and phrases were taken from the book, *A Call to a Deeper Love*. The family correspondence of parents of St. Therese of the Child Jesus (1863–1885).

The little queen was indeed well received that winters morning, and in the course of the day a poor waif rang timidly at the door of the happy home, and presented a paper bearing the following simple stanza: "Smile and swiftly grow; all beckons thee to joy, sweet love and tenderest care. Smile gladly at the dawn. Bud of an hour! For thou shalt be a stately Rose."

ABOUT THE AUTHOR

Barbara Hegger-Romero. Photograph by Gene Peach.

Barbara's roots run deep within the tradition of the Catholic faith. Even as a child, she was sensitive to the stirrings of the Holy Spirit. Whereby she had concern and compassion for other children. Therefore, instead of playing with dolls, she chose to cut out children's images from Sears catalogs for it enabled her to select clothing, toys, and other necessities for her imaginary orphanage. She would some years later write a prayer for abused and neglected children.

Meanwhile, having been inspired by the writings of St. Therese on love, Barbara developed a devotion to the saint who is also referred to as "The Little Flower."

Throughout, Barbara's life has made her presence known via the appearance of unexpected roses and other magical happenings. One such incident occurred when Barbara, having felt called to recount her journey after several years, reconnected with writer/screenwriter/producer/ Glenda Finn who amongst other things has created works that pay tribute to St. Therese. Glenda agreed to help Barbara following a dream in which she saw the book complete. Once Glenda described the cover and shared the title, things began to flow.

Soon Barbara's vivid recollections became more visual as she shared them with a writer known for her visual imagery. In the interim, the patron saint to both women continued to make her presence known in what began to resemble a Divine Tapestry.

Barbara was at one time a Lay Missionary under the direction of Fr. Stephen Valenta OFM Conv. Whereby she along with others traveled to Germany for World Youth Day in 2005.

The Catholic Youth Festival in Cologne was attended by over four hundred thousand youth from two hundred countries along with the Pope, Cardinals, and Bishops as well as six thousand reporters. An estimated one million people joined Pope Benedict XVI for the conclusion of the festival with an open-air mass in the village of Marienfeld, Germany.

Barbara having worked in the aviation industry has traveled extensively, where her visits to the pilgrimage sites satisfied her interest in the lives of saints. Although, when she arrived in New Mexico, she literally stumbled upon the humble pilgrimage site of "The Santuario de Chimayo." Their fate once again appeared to have intervened when she was asked to open a gift shop and invited to live at the historic Los Luceros, where she soon met her future husband, who like herself had numerous experiences where "The Little Flower" had made her presence known. A fascinating parallel exists within the fact that her husband's aunt entered the Carmelite monastery at the age of fifteen, like St. Therese of Lisieux France.

Whereby the Leaves Have Fallen beckons one to recall instances in their lives where angels and saints may well have intervened while manifesting miracles.

www.ingramcontent.com/pod-product-compliance
Lightning Source LLC
Chambersburg PA
CBHW080028180426
43195CB00053B/2868